The 22E Society

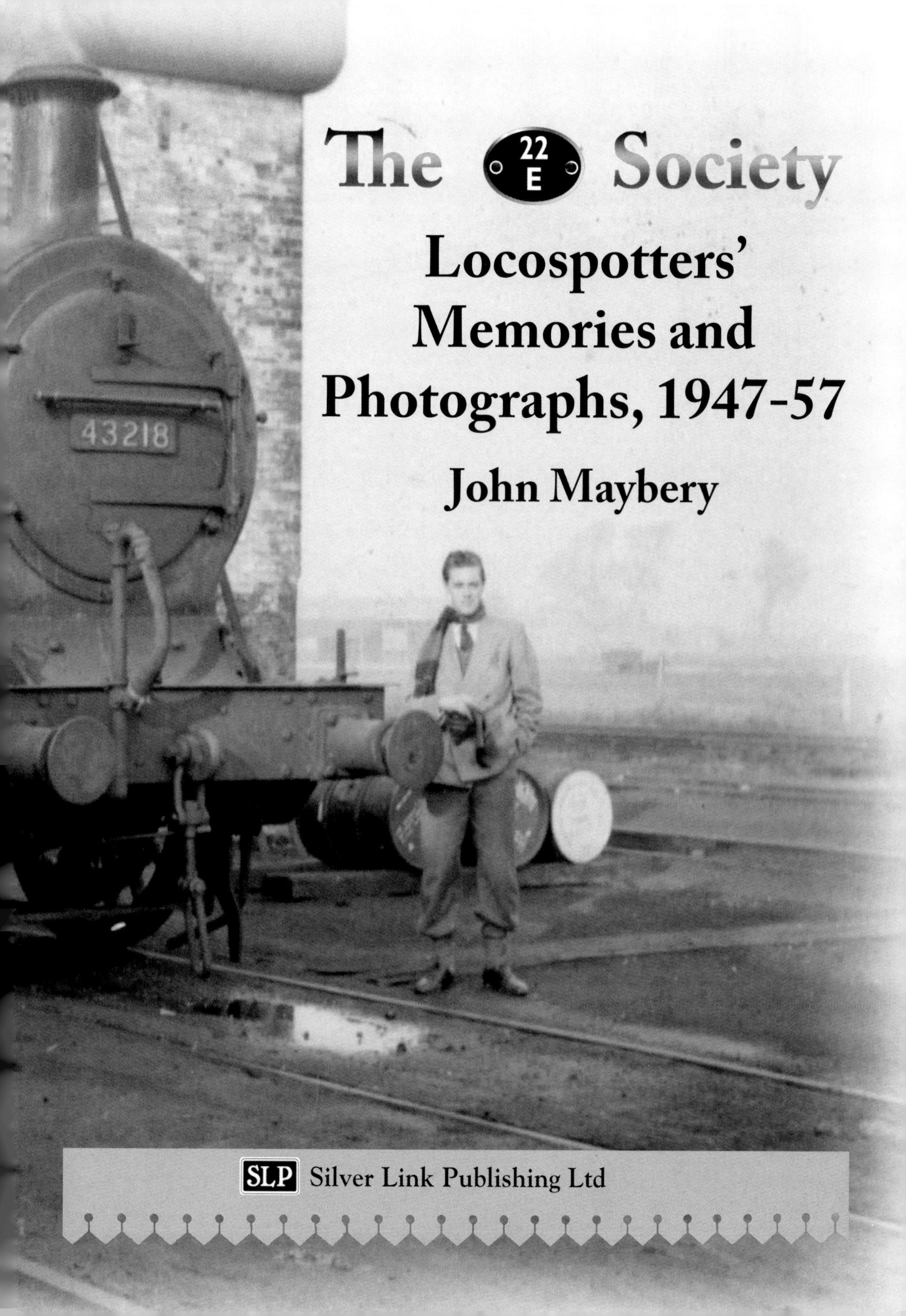
The 22E Society
Locospotters' Memories and Photographs, 1947-57
John Maybery
43218
SLP Silver Link Publishing Ltd

First published in 2011

British Library Cataloguing in Publication Data

A catalogue record for this book is available from the British Library.

ISBN 978 1 85794 389 4

Silver Link Publishing Ltd
The Trundle
Ringstead Road
Great Addington
Kettering
Northants NN14 4BW

Tel/Fax: 01536 330588
email: sales@nostalgiacollection.com
Website: www.nostalgiacollection.com

Printed and bound in the Czech Republic

Half title: Not quite as famous as Ivo Peters's Bentley, but we were lucky enough to have the use of Robin Ward's father's pre-war Rover saloon for some of our trips. Gathered around the car at Exeter on 26 March 1951 are four members of the 22E Society, from left to right Robin Ward (driver), Tony Hunt, John Madeley and Roy Medley.

Title page: Ex-Midland Railway 0-6-0 No 43218 stands in Highbridge loco yard alongside the water tower on 26 November 1950. 22E Society member John Madeley stands by the buffer beam.

Top right: A 'boys day out' – a cycle trip to Holford Glen in the Quantock Hills in April 1949. Sitting on a convenient gate near the village of Nether Stowey are (left to right) Roy Medley, Gerald Buncombe, John Madeley, Tony Hunt and John Maybery.

Right: Forty years on – growing older and older (with apologies to the famous public school song) – we sit on the same gate en route (by car) to the West Somerset Railway in June 1989. Left to right: John, Robin, Gerald, Roy and Tony.

Contents

Ivatt 2P 2-6-2T No 41241 stands alongside the primitive coaling arrangements at Highbridge loco, 22E, on 17 May 1951. The locomotive is now preserved on the Keighley & Worth Valley Railway and has also been released as an OO gauge model – a must for S&D modellers.

Introduction

The origins of the 22E Society were in the summer of 1946 in Highbridge, a small market town in Somerset. Highbridge was on the A38 trunk route to the South West, 25 miles south of Bristol and 7 miles north of Bridgwater. Even in the days of limited private car ownership, it was a holiday traffic bottleneck with many delays caused by the S&D level crossing on the main street. The closure of the S&D's Burnham branch in the 1960s and the construction of the M5 motorway turned Highbridge once more into a quiet market town.

22E was the code for the small locomotive shed at Highbridge, the smallest shed in the Bristol division of the LMS motive power department. An outpost of the LMS in the heart of Great Western territory, although it was only 25 miles from Bristol the route over LMS metals was via Evercreech Junction and Bath, a distance of some 60-70 miles. Highbridge shed was home to a small group of ex-Midland 0-4-4Ts and 0-6-0 tender engines, which handled the traffic between Evercreech and Burnham-on-Sea. The LMS line (always called the S&D by the local population) crossed the GWR line at Highbridge, and there were in effect two stations linked by a footbridge and at platform level.

Although having been born and living in Bristol, I spent many school holidays with my grandmother at Highbridge. I was aware of the S&D, as my late grandfather and several of his brothers-in-law had been employed on the S&D at Highbridge and other locations. My real interest in railways started in 1946 when I purchased my first *ABC* number book, and what better place to spot locomotives than at Highbridge station – like most stations it had its complement of 'locospotters'. Although we did not realise it at the time, this was the beginning of the 22E Society.

Highbridge Great Western station was a busy intermediate station on the Bristol-Exeter main line, with some eight to ten stopping trains per day, local pick-up goods and much through freight traffic. There was also a good deal of interchange freight traffic between the GWR and the S&D, with milk tanker traffic from the Express Dairy factory at Bason Bridge being transferred every evening at Highbridge to the West of England-London milk train. This was a slick operation, as within the space of 20 minutes or so the up main line would see this transfer, closely followed by the up mail train, which collected mail bags at speed from a lineside location, then a Plymouth-North of England express.

Overall, Highbridge was a busy station with two signal boxes, Highbridge West at the north end of the platforms controlling the main line and the S&D crossing to Burnham-on-Sea, and Highbridge East some 400 yards further north controlling the goods yard and sidings. Friday evenings were particularly busy as in season the local pigeon racing club would bring all its birds to be recorded and loaded into baskets and placed on a local stopping train for onward shipment to a North of England location.

All GWR traffic was usually in the hands of tender engines – the sight of a tank engine (apart from pannier tanks on the Taunton-Highbridge pick-up goods) was very rare. The majority of express passenger traffic was in the hands of 'Castles' and the occasional 'King' Class loco, while local passenger traffic was in the hands of 'Stars', 'Halls', 'Saints', and 2-6-0 'Moguls'. Freight traffic was usually handled by '28XX' 2-8-0s and, in the early years – 1946/47 – by the Swindon-built LMS 2-8-0s. They were gradually replaced by the much denigrated (by locospotters) 'Austerity' 2-8-0s. Occasionally we saw ageing 'ROD' 2-8-0s and 'Aberdare' 2-6-0s.

We passed from Great Western to British Railways ownership with very little noticeable change. The telephone in the booking office was now answered 'Highbridge, British Railways' and the S&D station was renamed Highbridge East. Locomotives started to appear with 'BRITISH RAILWAYS' on the tender side, and a number plate on the smokebox door (a useful aid to spotters on a dark evening).

By 1949/50 changes were taking place in our group of spotters – we were all leaving school and such things as work, higher education, National Service and girlfriends were taking priority over our latest locomotive sighting. Group contact had all but disappeared by 1954, and it was not until 1982 that the 22E Society was rejuvenated and our lifelong friendships renewed.

The content of the book has been split into five chapters covering the principal areas of interest and the history and ongoing activities of the 22E Society.

John Maybery
Barnstaple, North Devon

Arrival and departure at Highbridge: on 28 April 1951 0-4-4T No 58086 (formerly No 1423) arrives at the main platform with an Evercreech-Burnham train, while on the left sister engine No 58046 prepares to depart for Evercreech.

1. Bristol and the South West

These photographs cover the period 1949-52, with locations ranging from Bristol to Newton Abbot, including some branch lines in Devon.

No 4 platform at Bristol Temple Meads was an ideal venue for trainspotters, providing a good view of the Bath Road locomotive depot and all West of England arrivals and departures. Similarly the east end gave good views of departures to London Paddington and South Wales. Other traffic left from platforms 10-11 (if I remember correctly), with departures to Birmingham, Derby and the north; motive power was usually provided by 'Jubilees' and 'Black 5s' and occasionally the odd 'Patriot' or double-headed Midland Compounds.

Trips to other location such as Taunton or Exeter usually started from Highbridge – a day return ticket was good value for money. On several occasions we made use of Holiday Runabout tickets; two tickets at 15 shillings each purchased at Highbridge and Exeter gave us a week's travel throughout Somerset, Devon and over the Tamar Bridge to Saltash in Cornwall.

Most of the photographs in this chapter were taken by myself using, by present-day standards, two very basic cameras, a Coronet Cub with a 1/25th shutter, apertures of f8 and f11, and a film size approximating to 35mm, the other a folding Brownie with speeds of 1/25th and 1/50th and f6.3 lenses and a 620 size film.

On Saturday 12 February 1949 'Castle' Class No 7011 *Banbury Castle* stands outside Bristol Bath Road loco painted in apple green livery, one of British Railways' experimental express locomotive liveries. It did not suit Great Western engines and was very short-lived. Note the 'British Railways' insignia on the tender. Built in June 1948, *Banbury Castle* was at this time only eight months old.

Above: '2884' Class 2-8-0 No 3811 is just north of Bridgwater station with a load of coal empties on 9 April 1949. Built in 1939 as part of lot No 328, No 3811 is ten years old and has some 14 years more life before scrapping in 1963.

Below: 'Star' Class four-cylinder 4-6-0 No 4041 *Prince of Wales* stands at the east end of Bristol Temple Meads No 6 platform with a Bath-Swindon stopping train on 30 April 1949. Now relegated from her former express duties, No 4041 was scrapped in 1951.

Above: '5100' Class 2-6-2 T No 4143 stands at No 2 platform at Bristol Temple Meads with an all-stations train for Weston-super-Mare on 7 May 1949. No 4143 had only just been allocated to Bristol Bath Road (BRD), an early indication that the '45XX' Class tanks were being gradually withdrawn.

Below: 'Hall' Class 4-6-0 No 5924 *Dinton Hall* stands at No 9 platform at Bristol Temple Meads with a parcels train for the London area on 17 June 1949.

'Grange' Class 4-6-0 No 6804 *Brockington Grange* takes on water at Bristol Temple Meads No 7 platform on the same day. None of these engines were preserved, but rumours circulated among enthusiasts that many of the class were mothballed as part of a strategic reserve – dream on! Fortunately a new-build No 6880 is now under way at the Llangollen Railway.

'Modified Hall' '6959' Class No 7904 *Fountains Hall* stands on the through road adjacent to No 9 platform at Bristol Temple Meads on 23 July 1949. At the time of this photograph No 7904 was only three months old and still looked spick and span.

'43XX' Class No 9311 stands at Bristol Temple Meads No 7 platform on 28 July 1949. The last 20 of this class, Nos 9300-9319, were built in 1932 by C. B. Collett with 'Castle'-type cabs, which I believe greatly enhanced their appearance.

'Hall' Class No 4968 *Shotton Hall* stands at Bridgwater General down starter signal with an afternoon Bristol-Exeter semi-fast service on 30 July 1949.

Above: On the same day '28XX' Class No 2803, in ex-works condition, was photographed in the same spot with a down parcels train.

Bottom left and above: On 20 August 1949 'Castle' Class No 5023 *Brecon Castle* stands on the through line at Newton Abbot station with a Paddington-Plymouth express. This was not a scheduled passenger stop and the train is waiting for a pilot engine to be attached for assistance over the South Devon banks to Plymouth. The second photograph shows that 'Manor' Class 4-6-0 No 7801 *Anthony Manor* was the pilot engine used.

Churchward-built '43XX' Class No 5384 waits at Bristol Temple Meads No 4 platform with a stopping train for Taunton and Exeter on 31 August 1949.

On Saturday 3 September 1949 'Modified Hall' Class No 6978 *Haroldstone Hall* is on the same parcels train as seen in the upper picture on page 11.

'14XX' Class 0-4-2T No 5809 was acting as the east-end station pilot at Bristol Temple Meads on 3 September 1949. The locomotives in the '58XX' series differed from those in the '14XX' series in that they were not fitted for auto-car service.

On the same day two 'old stagers' were seen at Bristol Temple Meads. 'Saint' Class 4-6-0 No 2955 *Tortworth Court* is standing at No 4 platform with a train for Weston-super-Mare, while 'Dean Goods' 0-6-0 No 2444 is at No 2 platform with a train for the Portishead branch.

On 11 September '57XX' Class 0-6-0PT No 3731 stands at the east end of No 4 platform at Bristol Temple Meads while undertaking pilot duties. No 3731 was one of the large-cab variants built in 1937.

'Modified Hall' Class No 6994 *Baggrave Hall* is also seen at No 4 platform at Bristol Temple Meads with the 11.30am Bristol to Weston-super-Mare train on 1 October 1949.

'14XX' Class No 5813 undertakes duties as the Bristol Temple Meads west-end station pilot on 4 February 1950. No 5813 was one of the class not fitted with boiler top-feed apparatus.

'57XX' Class 0-6-0PT No 8713 waits to leave Bristol St Philips Marsh MPD with a load of empty coal wagons on 1 March 1950. Access to the shed was reasonably easy for enthusiasts – climb up a flight of steps from the road, do not attempt to wander into the shed buildings and generally try and remain unobtrusive. On a Sunday morning the shed area was usually crammed with locos, some 20-30 being visible from the top of the steps.

'2021' Class 0-6-0PT No 2072 is acting as station pilot at the west end of Bristol Temple Meads on 11 March 1950. This locomotive was, I believe, sold out of service to the National Smelting Co, Avonmouth, to supplement its fleet of ageing locos.

'2251' Class 0-6-0 No 2225 is seen just north of Highbridge station on a Taunton-Bristol local goods train. The photograph was taken from Bristol Bridge on the A38 on the northern outskirts of Highbridge on 25 March 1950.

'Grange' Class 4-6-0 No 6815 *Frilford Grange* stands at Highbridge station's down platform with a Bristol-Taunton stopping train on 29 April 1950.

'Castle' Class No 5022 *Wigmore Castle* awaits departure from Bristol Temple Meads with a South Wales train on Saturday 1 July 1950.

'Hall' Class No 5925 *Eastcote Hall* backs down to No 9 platform at Bristol Temple Meads to couple onto a train for Paddington on 1 July 1950. Moments later London Midland Region Class 5 4-6-0 No 44808 runs into the station past No 5925 with a through train for the West of England.

'Castle' Class No 5078 *Lysander* departs from Highbridge with a stopping train to Bristol on Saturday 19 August 1950. The Somerset & Dorset branch line to Burnham-on-Sea can be seen in the top left of the photograph.

On the same day another 'Castle', No 4096 *Highclere Castle*, passes Bridgwater's up goods siding at the head of a goods train, a fairly unusual working for a 'Castle' locomotive at this time.

'2021' Class 0-6-0PT No 2038 shunts at Bridgwater top yard, also on 19 August 1950.

On 27 August 1950 '72XX' 2-8-2T No 7244 approaches Highbridge from the north with a heavy goods train. Large tank engines were very rare in this location and the sight of a 2-8-2T was certainly the 'cop' of the day.

'King' Class 4-6-0 No 6015 *King Richard III* awaits departure from Bristol Temple Meads with an Exeter-Plymouth express on 2 September 1950. This photograph clearly shows the massive size of a 'King' boiler compared to the 'Castles' and 'Stars'.

On that day '4575' Class No 5558 was the Temple Meads station pilot. A large number of '4500' and '4575' Class locos were allocated to Bristol Bath Road, mainly employed on the Avonmouth/ Severn Beach, Cheddar Valley and Portishead services.

'Saint' Class No 2931 *Arlington Court* leaves Bristol Temple Meads No 2 platform with an Saturday all-stations train for Weston-super-Mare on 2 September 1950.

'Castle' Class 4-6-0 No 4084 *Aberystwyth Castle* runs into Bristol Bath Road loco on the same day, and at the same spot we see 'Star' Class 4-6-0 No 4035 *Queen Charlotte* departing with a train for Weston-super-Mare. By this time the 'Stars' were being relegated to secondary passenger duties.

Gas turbine locomotive No 18000 prepares to run into Bath Road loco after bringing in the 9.00am Paddington-Bristol express on a wet 14 October 1950.

A snowy scene at Bristol Temple Meads on 16 December 1950 as 'Hall' Class No 6923 *Croxteth Hall* departs from No 5 platform with an empty stock train en route to the carriage sidings at Malago Vale.

On the same snowy day 'Hall' Class No 5974 *Wallsworth Hall* backs additional coaches onto a South Wales train at the east end of Temple Meads.

'Castle' Class No 4075 *Cardiff Castle* moves out of Bristol Bath Road loco 'coaled and watered' ready for her next turn of duty on Saturday 27 January 1951.

'Hall' Class No 5993 *Kirby Hall* runs into Bristol Bath Road loco on 27 January 1951.

'County' Class No 1005 *County of Devon* pulls out of Bristol with an empty stock train for Malago Vale, also on 27 January 1951. In the background can be seen a 'Saint' Class 4-6-0.

On the same day as the pictures opposite, 'Castle' Class No 5021 *Whittington Castle* leaves No 2 platform at Bristol Temple Meads with a down parcels train. The 'Saint' is still in the background.

A week later, on 3 February, 'Castle' Class No 4084 *Aberystwyth Castle* speeds through Bridgwater with a Penzance-Wolverhampton express, while in the late afternoon sunshine '28XX' Class No 2881 approaches from the north with a down goods train. In the left background is the tall chimney stack of the British Cellophane Company – the industrial process in this factory produced the most nauseating smell of sulphur compounds, so you could always tell when you were approaching Bridgwater!

Above: On Saturday 24 March 1951 'Hall' Class No 4973 *Sweeney Hall* pounds her way up Wellington bank prior to entering Whiteball Tunnel, which marks the boundary between Somerset and Devon.

Opposite below and above: 'County' Class No 1021 *County of Montgomery* leaves the tunnel for the run down the bank and on to Taunton with an empty stock train. The locomotive has a full head of steam but is minus its safety valve casing. It is followed by 'Castle' Class No 5037 *Monmouth Castle* with the 8.45am Plymouth-Liverpool express.

'43XX' Class 2-6-0 No 7316 exits Whiteball Tunnel with an Exeter-Bristol train on the same day, 24 March 1951. Sited on the bank is an old carriage being used as a gangers' hut – if still in existence it would be a preservation dream find!

Travelling in the other direction, '28XX' Class No 2875 plods slowly up Wellington bank with a down mixed goods. It is being assisted at the rear by a '41XX' 2-6-2 tank, attached at Wellington sidings.

Finally that day we see '8750' Class 0-6-0PT No 3736 leaving Highbridge down loop after completing shunting/transfer duties on the Taunton-Highbridge-Taunton afternoon pick-up goods. This turn complemented the Bristol West depot-Highbridge pick-up goods, which worked as far as Highbridge every morning.

'Castles' at Exeter St David's on 26 March 1951. In the first picture Nos 5039 *Rhuddlan Castle* and 5027 *Farleigh Castle* are double-heading the 11.00am Paddington-Plymouth express, while the second view shows, on the left, Southern Region 'West Country' 'Pacific' No 34017 *Ilfracombe* with a train from the Barnstaple branch, preparing to start eastwards up the steep bank to Exeter Central, and 'Castle' Class No 5047 *Earl of Dartmouth* heading westwards to Newton Abbot and Plymouth.

Locomotive movements at Bristol Bath Road shed on Saturday 7 April 1951: '4575' Class No 5528 repositions 'County' Class No 1002 *County of Berks and* an unidentified '4575' Class tank. The second picture shows 'Dean Goods' '2301' Class No 2322, 'out of steam', being repositioned; these engines were often employed on the Portishead and Cheddar Valley lines with a 'B Set' of coaching stock.

'Star' Class No 4043 *Prince Henry* moves out of Bristol Bath Road loco on the same day.

'2884' Class No 3864 passes through Bristol Temple Meads with a down goods. Goods trains at Temple Meads were quite unusual as most good traffic took the avoiding line to the rear of Bath Road shed.

Above: Finally on 7 April 1951 we see 'Castle' Class No 5082 *Swordfish* departing from Bristol Temple Meads No 4 platform on the last leg of a Paddington-Weston-super-Mare express.

Right: Two weeks later we are back at Temple Meads. On 21 April 1951 'Saint' Class No 2950 *Taplow Court* waits at the exit from Bath Road loco prior to backing on to the 4.08pm Bristol-Taunton all-stations train, then is seen leaving with the train from No 2 platform.

A new class of locomotive for Bristol: this was the first appearance of a '61XX' 2-6-2T, in this case No 6107, standing outside Bath Road loco on 21 April 1951 after reallocation from Old Oak Common.

On 29 April 1951 'Hall' Class No 6957 *Norcliffe Hall* passes Highbridge goods yard with a down goods train. The S&D branch line to Burnham-on-Sea goes off on the left.

On Saturday 29 September 1951 we witnessed a rare class of locomotive for this line, as Standard 'Pacific' No 70022 *Tornado* ran into Bridgwater station with the 1.00pm Plymouth-Manchester train. It was only when I was looking at these photographs recently that I realised that one of the houses in the background was the home of my future wife, Joyce (five years in the future). In the second picture *Tornado* awaits the 'right away' from Bridgwater station.

'Hall' Class No 5931 *Hatherley Hall* shows a good turn of speed as she passes Highbridge up refuge siding on an afternoon express to Bristol, also on 29 September 1951. A '28XX' 2-8-0 is waiting in the siding.

On Saturday 3 November 1951 we are back at Bristol, and photograph 'County' Class No 1028 *County of Warwick* standing outside Bath Road loco.

'King' Class No 6014 *King Henry VII* runs out of Bath Road loco and proceeds to No 9 platform to head a Bristol-Paddington express on 3 November 1951.

'Castle' Class No 5025 *Chirk Castle* gleams brightly in the pale winter sun at No 4 platform with a Paddington to Weston-super-Mare train on the same day.

In the spring of 1952 Standard 'Pacific' No 70023 *Venus* runs into Bristol Temple Meads with the down 'Bristolian'. For many years this train was in the hands of 'Kings' and 'Castles' – times are changing!

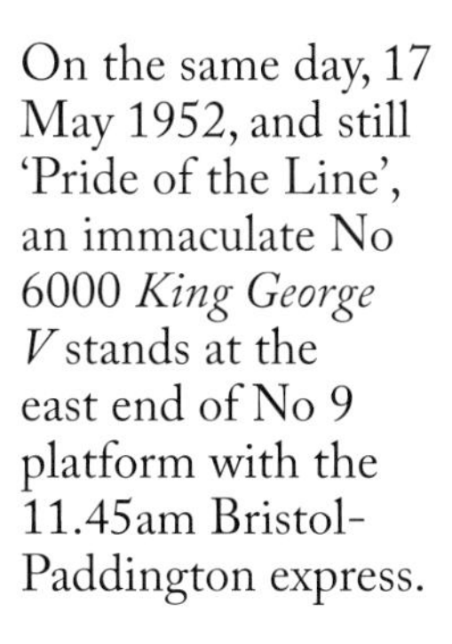

On the same day, 17 May 1952, and still 'Pride of the Line', an immaculate No 6000 *King George V* stands at the east end of No 9 platform with the 11.45am Bristol-Paddington express.

London Midland Region interlopers at Temple Meads on 17 May 1952: 2-6-0 No 43046 passes through with a transfer goods for Bristol West depot. To 'Western' eyes, No 43046, with its huge double chimney and high running plate, looked ugly, but nevertheless very functional. The second picture shows Fowler 0-6-0 4F No 44537 departing from Bristol Temple Meads with a parcels train for the Midland Region.

Also on 17 May 1952 '8750' Class 0-6-0PT No 9655 stands at Bristol Temple Meads No 14 platform with a train for Severn Beach. No 14 and the adjacent platform were part of the original Brunel station. The Severn Beach line was the busiest of the local lines serving Avonmouth Docks and the large Zinc Smelter at St Andrews Road, Avonmouth.

A mid-morning scene at Tiverton Junction on Tuesday 5 August 1952. '14XX' Class 0-4-2T No 1468 runs in with an auto-car working from Tiverton Town, and is seen again in the second pictures in the bay with the return working as a 28XX 2-8-0 stands in the up platform with an up goods. The line climbs from here to Whiteball Tunnel and down Wellington Bank to Taunton and Bristol.

'14XX' Class, No 1439, runs into Heathfield station with an auto-car on the Newton Abbot-Moretonhampstead branch, also on 5 August 1952.

End of the line: Another 0-4-2T No 1429 with the 9.10am Tiverton Junction to Hemyock branch train stands in Hemyock station on 5 August 1952. Milk tanker traffic was taken down this line every day to be connected to one of the West Country-London milk trains.

'14XX' Class No 1470 stands in Totnes station with the Ashburton branch auto-car train on 5 August 1952, probably not long after being overhauled, as it looks immaculate in British Railways mixed-traffic livery. No 1470 is seen again setting off for Ashburton while '51XX' Class 2-6-2T No 5108 waits in the siding prior to acting as a banker on Rattery Bank.

A memorial to a forgotten railway – the Moretonhampstead & South Devon. This stone was standing in Moretonhampstead station yard. I wonder where it is now – preserved, I hope.

The following day, Wednesday 6 August 1952, 'Castle' Class No 7029 *Clun Castle* stands in Newton Abbot station with the down 'Devonian'. In the background is Southern Region 'West Country' 4-6-2 No 34014 *Budleigh Salterton*.

On the same day Southern Region 'Battle of Britain' Class No 34062 *17 Squadron* pulls away from Exeter St David's for the steep climb to Exeter Central with a train from the Ilfracombe-Barnstaple line.

On Thursday 7 August 1952 '44XX' Class 2-6-2T No 4401 passes through Newton Abbot station with a local pick-up goods. In the background stand the buildings of the locomotive repair factory.

'4575' Class 2-6-2T No 5557 stands outside Newton Abbot locomotive dept. In the background is the crane of the locally based breakdown train.

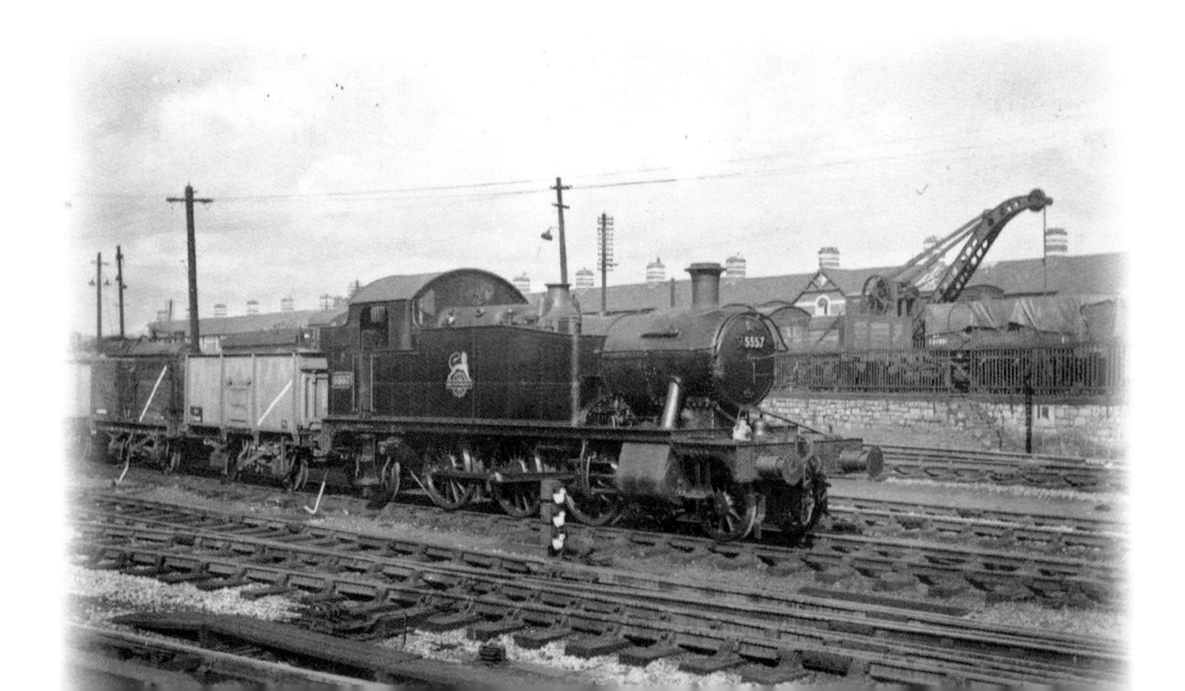

The third 'Prairie' tank seen that day was '51XX' Class No 5140, seen here leaving Newton Abbot locomotive depot.

Another 'Prairie' seen on 7 August 1952 was '4575' Class No 4587, waiting at Kingsbridge with the 2.00pm train for Brent. The Kingsbridge branch was a very busy summer route, especially with visitors for Salcombe; it connected with the main line at Brent, between Newton Abbot and Plymouth.

On the same day 'King' Class No 6024 *King Edward I* stands in Taunton station with a Plymouth-London express.

This was the limit of our Holiday Runabout tickets – Saltash station in Cornwall. The Royal Albert Bridge crossing the River Tamar can be seen in the background.

Not a Somerset & Dorset scene: Midland Region 4F No 44056 stands in Highbridge down loop with the empty stock from a Midlands-Weston-super-Mare excursion on Wednesday 3 September 1952.

Below and opposite top: The following Saturday, the 6th, we were at Bristol Temple Meads and photographed 'King' Class No 6000 *King George V* backing onto the 11.45am Bristol-Paddington express at No 9 platform. The locomotive is involved in some form of test as she

is fitted with the Great Western self-weighing tender. We also saw 'Castle' Class No 5066 *Wardour Castle* running in with the down 'Bristolian'.

On 6 September 1952 Midland Region Class 5 No 44919 has just arrived at Temple Meads with a through train for the West of England. On the adjacent line '45XX' Class No 4535 is the west-end station pilot.

'County' Class No 1011 *County of Warwick* stands at Bristol Temple Meads No 2 platform with the 11.05am stopping train to Taunton on 6 September 1952. On the adjacent platform a '4575' Class 2-6-2T is at the head of a train for the Portishead line.

Gas turbine locomotive No 18000 stands on the through line at Temple Meads on the same occasion, after bringing a morning express down from Paddington, which was a regular duty for this locomotive.

'Grange' Class No 6868 *Penrhos Grange* pulls out of Highbridge down loop with a Bristol-Taunton stopping train on 18 October 1952. The train had been put back into the loop to allow a down express to pass.

End of a holiday: 'Castle' Class No 4086 *Builth Castle* waits to depart from Penzance station with the northbound 'Cornishman' on 9 August 1954.

The end of another Cornish holiday – *Builth Castle* is seen again at the head of the up 'Cornishman' at Penzance station in May 1958. I was undertaking my two years National Service at the time and had a leave pass to travel from Bramley (Hants) to Penzance via Reading and Westbury (Wilts). However, I needed to travel via Bristol to meet up with my wife and lost count of the number of guards and ticket collectors I had to convince that I was not on the wrong train. By the time I returned to Bramley the ticket had been punched so many times it was virtually all holes!

The next two photographs were taken by Tony Hunt. Tony travelled to school at Weston-super-Mare every day from Highbridge and often took his camera with him. This photograph shows '28XX' Class No 2826 passing northwards through Weston- super-Mare with a freight train. The best date I can give for this photograph is 1947.

The second photograph shows 'Saint'

Class No 2929 *Saint Stephen* standing at Brent Knoll station with a down stopping train. Brent Knoll was a small station between Weston-super-Mare and Highbridge and a long walk from the village of the same name. Once again I can only date this to 1947.

The last five photographs are strictly outside the date period of this book, but I think that diesel power had made little impact on the Bristol-Taunton line at this time. They were all taken on one afternoon in the spring of 1962. The first could have been taken in the mid-1940s when wartime, Great Western-built LMS 8F 2-8-0s were an everyday sight. No 48456 is near Uphill Junction on the Bristol-Taunton line at the head of a goods train.

Another goods train, this time at Worle Junction, sees an unidentified '2884' Class 2-8-0 hauling a mixed load of wagons. The first four wagons are a North Eastern Region brake-van, a coach and two low-loaders carrying earth-moving equipment.

'County' Class No 1005 *County of Devon* proceeds northwards on an Exeter-Bristol train at Worle Junction.

'Hall' Class No 4953 *Pitchford Hall* draws into Highbridge up platform with a Taunton-Bristol train.

The wind of change: 'Warship' Class diesel-hydraulic D823 *Hermes* heads towards Bristol at Worle Junction.

2. South Wales Sheds

Access to GWR/Western Region sheds was always difficult on a casual basis. The odd shed foreman would turn a blind eye if you were lucky, but most of them ensured that their domain was a 'no-go area' to the casual spotter.

There was, however, an organisation called the British Locomotive Society (BLS), which flourished in the 1940s and 1950s. Based in Birmingham, it produced books of shed allocations for all regions and these were updated by regular newsletters. One of the attractions of membership was that the Society was able to obtain permits to visit locomotive sheds, usually on a Sunday. These visits were always well patronised and, depending on location, would cover five or six sheds in a day. A coach-load of enthusiasts would descend on a shed and within a space of some 45 minutes every locomotive would be noted, recorded and photographed as appropriate.

The South Wales sheds were of particular interest to someone living in the South West, as they were home to a myriad of locomotives that never came south of the Severn. In particular, the wide range of tank engines that came into Great Western ownership in 1923 were the main attractions.

I went on three of these trips, two starting at Cardiff and the other at Swansea. The second Cardiff trip in particular still brings back many memories. It involved meeting at Cardiff station on a Sunday morning at 7.00am for a cooked breakfast in the station Refreshment Rooms. However, the only train that could get you there in time from Bristol left just after midnight, arriving in Cardiff at about 1.00am. This meant trying to sleep on a freezing cold platform bench, as the waiting rooms were locked overnight.

The Swansea trip was far more comfortable. I had an aunt and uncle who lived there, so had the benefit of an overnight bed. Looking back on these trips, my only regret is that I did not take more photographs.

The first British Locomotive Society visit took place on Sunday 14 June 1950. At Newport Ebbw Junction loco is '42XX' 2-8-0T No 4247, one of the class variants with outside steam pipes.

'2021' Class 0-6-0PT No 2122 is also seen at Ebbw Junction. Build in the period 1897-1905 to a William Dean design, there were more than 100 of these locomotives still in service at this time.

'15XX' Class 0-6-0PT No 1507 was photographed at Newport Dock loco. Mainly employed at Paddington on empty stock movements and rated 'Red' for weight restriction purposes, it was quite a surprise to find No 1507 this far west on lightly loaded docks lines.

'56XX' Class 0-6-2T No 6689 is at Severn Tunnel Junction loco. Severn Tunnel Junction had a large hump shunting yard, and the hump shunter was an ex-Brecon & Merthyr 0-6-2T, my first glimpse of a pre-Grouping locomotive.

We saw '4575' Class 2-6-2T No 5538 at Gloucester loco. This was the last port of call on this trip, and looking back I am surprised at the small number of photographs taken – maybe funds were low.

The second BLS trip was on Sunday 8 July 1951, and the first shed on the itinerary was Cardiff Canton, where ex-Alexandra Docks & Railway 2-6-2T No 1205 was observed. Built by Hawthorn Leslie in 1920, it was therefore only 30 years old.

Ex-Rhymney Railway Class 'A1' 0-6-2T No 67 was seen at Cardiff East Dock loco. It was still in its original form apart from the addition of a GWR safety valve casing.

No 63 was another Rhymney Railway 'A1' 0-6-2T, as rebuilt with a Great Western taper boiler and fittings. These were powerful locomotives, with a tractive effort in excess of the '56XX' Class.

Also at Cardiff East Dock loco were '2021' Class 0-6-0PT No 2147, one of the half-cab variants of the class, and ex-Cardiff Railway 0-6-2T No 155, built in 1908 and rebuilt by the Great Western in 1928.

Class '44XX' 2-6-2T No 4404, designed by G. J. Churchward in 1904, is seen here at Tondu loco. This small class was quite widely distributed throughout the system.

'57XX' Class 0-6-0PT No 3668 is at the head of a local passenger train approaching Tondu station. A wartime build from March 1940, No 3668 was one of the '8750' series with the larger cab.

'42XX' Class 2-8-0T No 4241 is on the turntable at Duffryn Yard-Port Talbot loco.

Two locomotives spotted at Danygraig loco were '1101' Class 0-4-0T No 1105, built by the Avonside Engine Co in 1926 but designed by C. B. Collett, and Peckett-built 0-4-0ST No 1151, taken into Great Western service at the Grouping from contractors Powsland & Mason.

At Aberdare were '42XX' Class 2-8-0T No 4251, standing on the coaling line.

Finally, at Abercynon loco we saw ex-Taff Vale Railway Class 'O4' 0-6-2T No 293 in its rebuilt form. Abercynon loco carried the shed prefix 'CV', denoting that it was one of the Cardiff Valley sheds.

Another ex-Taff Vale Railway locomotive at Abercynon was Class 'A' 0-6-2T No 356, as rebuilt in 1924 from the original TVR design of 1914. With driving wheels of 5ft 3in they were probably designed for passenger working.

The third and final BLS trip was on Sunday 27 April 1952, starting from Swansea. Standing outside Swansea's Landore loco is Collett '2251' Class 0-6-0 No 2273.

One of the later-built '42XX' Class 2-8-0Ts, No 5249, was also seen at Landore.

'56XX' Class No 6695 pushes coal wagons up to the coaling tip at Landore.

'43XX' Class 2-6-0 No 5356 stands in front of one of Landore's 'Castle' Class allocation, which were used on the Swansea-Paddington services.

An interior shot of Llanelly loco roundhouse. The locomotives on view are, left to right, 0-6-0PTs No 9743 and No 9468, 2-8-0T No 5261 and 0-6-0PT No 1609.

2167

2167

Our next port of call was Burry Port loco, west of Swansea. Standing outside the shed was ex-Burry Port & Gwendraeth Valley outside-cylinder 0-6-0T No 2167. Built in 1927 by Hudswell Clarke, it was subsequently rebuilt by the Great Western. Standing next to No 2167 was '2021' Class 0-6-0PT No 2069, and the third picture shows another ex-BP&GVR 0-6-0T, No 2162.

Moving further west, we visited Carmarthen loco and saw '2021' Class 0-6-0PT No 2111; this class variant has a very basic full cab.

A contrast in locomotive power is 'Castle' Class No 7017 *G. J. Churchward*, built in 1948 and with another 11 years' service left. The 4-6-0 is standing outside Carmarthen loco ready for a Monday morning run to London Paddington.

Another '2021' Class pannier at Carmarthen was No 2069, looking rather abandoned against the buffer stops.

Also at Carmarthen was '14XX' Class 0-4-2T No 5819, one of the class not equipped for auto-car working and not fitted with top-feed apparatus.

Finally at Carmarthen was one of the Hawksworth replacements for the '2021' Class, '16XX' Class 0-6-0PT No 1613.

The furthest point west on this trip was Whitland loco, where '16XX' Class No 1602 was photographed.

'45XX' Class 2-6-2T No 4506 was one of the early locos in this class built with inside steam pipes. No 5549, a member of the '4575' Class with enlarged side tanks, can be seen behind.

Farewell to Wales: another '16XX' Class tank photographed at Whitland was No 1606.

3. Photographs of the late John Madeley

John joined the GWR as an apprentice in the Signal & Telegraph Department in 1947 and spent his early working days in the Taunton/Bristol area followed by a spell in the Drawing Office at Reading. It was in the Drawing Office that he met Avril, the lady who was to become his wife.

Even in BR days he was a Great Western man through and through, and whenever possible maintained the traditions of the Great Western Railway. I can well remember meeting him in the 1970s – he was driving an S&T van with a BR logo on the side, underneath which he had applied a small GWR coat of arms, probably not noticed by many people. The spirit of the Great Western lived on!

On his retirement he joined the West Somerset Railway as its Signal Engineer, and many of the signalling projects on the WSR are a fitting memorial to his very professional approach to the job. Unfortunately John was the first member of the 22E Society to pass away, in 2003.

In his early working days John always took his camera to work and photographed locomotives at many trackside locations. I have selected some 60 of his photographs, the best of which I feel is the shot of the LNER 'A4' 'Pacific' at Taunton during the locomotive exchange trials. Unfortunately it has not been possible to date many of the views, other than to say that they were taken in the period 1947-52.

I am grateful to Avril for giving me permission to use her late husband's photographs.

One of John's photographs depicts the 22E Society on a spotting trip. We had shed permits to visit Bristol St Philips Marsh and the Midland shed at Barrow Road (22A). Pictured at the former, standing beside '28XX' Class No 2838 are, left to right, Roy Medley, a non-member, Tony Hunt, John Maybery and Gerald Buncombe.

'Hall' Class 4-6-0 No 4917 *Crosswood Hall* passes Highbridge's up refuge siding with the early evening West of England-London milk train.

Another 'Hall', No 6918 *Standon Hall*, awaits the 'right away' at Highbridge's down platform.

Three more views of trains on the down (southbound) line at Highbridge. The first is a pre-nationalisation shot of 'County' Class 4-6-0 No 1028 *County of Warwick* standing at the down platform with a Bristol-Taunton stopping train.

Built after the war in 1947, Collett '2251' Class No 3215 passes through the station with a down local goods train. The locomotive is coupled to an ex-ROD tender from a scrapped '30XX' Class 2-8-0.

'Castle' Class No 5077 *Fairey Battle* stands at the down platform with a Bristol-Taunton stopping train. No 5077 was shedded at Taunton, and appeared for trainspotters with regular monotony twice a day.

Another everyday sighting at Highbridge was Taunton-shedded 'Star' Class No 4056 *Princess Margaret*, which worked a Taunton-Bristol train in the morning and the reverse turn in the early evening. Standing at Highbridge down platform, No 4056 was the last of the class, withdrawn in October 1957.

ROD 2-8-0 No 3018 passes through the station with a down goods. Originally built to a Great Central design, these First World War engines, on acquisition, were 'Westernised' with a safety valve casing, top-feed and chimney .

A lowly duty for the 'Pride of the Line': 'King' Class No 6000 *King George V* stands at Highbridge's down platform with a Bristol-Taunton stopping train.

GWR '57XX' Class 0-6-0PT No 9765 stands at Highbridge down loop. Built in 1935, No 9765 was one of the '8750' series with the improved cab.

Two goods trains pull away from Highbridge down loop: the first is headed by unnamed 'Bulldog' Class 4-4-0 No 3383, and the second by '43XX' Class 'Mogul' No 5356.

This pre-nationalisation shot shows 'Dean Goods' 0-6-0 No 2322 passing Yatton with a local goods train. Yatton was between Highbridge and Bristol on the main line, and was the junction for the Cheddar Valley line, which at its far end connected with the Paddington-West of England line at Witham Friary, and also for the short branch line to Clevedon. The Weston, Clevedon & Portishead Light Railway was close to the Clevedon terminus, and one of its locomotives became No 5 *Portishead* in the GWR stock book (see page 92).

'Hall' Class No 6900 *Abney Hall* is seen at Claverham, near Yatton, with an up goods.

'Dean Goods' 0-6-0 No 2340 passes Bristol Temple Meads East signal box.

'Hall' Class No 4996 *Eden Hall* stands at Bristol St Philips Marsh loco on 30 January 1948.

'County' Class No 1014 *County of Glamorgan* is seen outside Bristol Bath Road loco.

Stanier 2-6-2T No 40174 is pictured at Bristol Barrow Road loco. This engine rarely appeared at Bristol Temple Meads, as it normally worked the Midland Region line from Bristol St Philips to Bath Green Park.

LMS Johnson 0-6-0T No 1874 (not yet renumbered) stands at the rear of Barrow Road loco. Three 22E members are standing at the extreme right of the photograph.

Some 4 miles south of Highbridge on the main line towards Bridgwater is Puriton cutting, where 'Castle' Class No 5069 *Isambard Kingdom Brunel* is seen heading a Bristol-Taunton stopping train.

Another 'Castle', No 7000 *Viscount Portal*, approaches Bridgwater from the north with the 9.15am Liverpool-Plymouth express. In the background is the overbridge carrying the Somerset & Dorset Edington Junction to Bridgwater branch line.

Two down goods trains are seen at almost the same spot, headed by '43XX' Class 'Mogul' No 5739 (*above*) and '2884' Class 2-8-0 No 2895, passing under the Bridgwater S&D branch line overbridge.

'Castle' Class No 7011 *Banbury Castle* is just north of Bridgwater with a down express.

'County' Class No 1011 *County of Chester* stands at Bridgwater's down platform with a Bristol-Exeter train on the afternoon of 9 April 1949.

Shunting at Bridgwater Top Yard shunting spur is '2021' Class 0-6-0PT No 2038.

Passing the British Cellophane factory at Bridgwater with an up goods is 'WD' 'Austerity' 2-8-0 No 77077, which is still numbered in the wartime WD system before being renumbered in the BR 90XXX series.

Durston was an intermediate station on the West of England line between Bridgwater and Taunton. The two locomotives photographed there are '47XX' Class 2-8-0 No 4706 and, in the station, 'Grange' Class No 6816 *Frankton Grange*.

'Grange' Class 4-6-0 No 6870 *Bodicote Grange* passes Taunton East Junction with a stopping train to Bristol Temple Meads.

'1501' Class 0-6-0PT No 2708 stands by Taunton East Loop signal box. The '1501' Class was designed by Dean/Armstrong in the period 1879/1896 and later rebuilt by G. J. Churchward.

Two 'King' Class 4-6-0s, Nos 6006 *King George I* and 6025 *King Henry III*, stand at Taunton station at the head of Plymouth-Paddington expresses.

In the early months of nationalisation, but still in full GW regalia, 'King' Class No 6010 *King Charles I* waits at Taunton's main up platform on 27 March 1948. The locomotive on the adjacent line is '2251' Class 0-6-0 No 2261.

During the locomotive exchange trials of July 1948, Eastern Region 'A4' Class 4-6-2 No 60033 *Seagull* attracts the crowds at Taunton station with a Plymouth-Paddington express. On the adjacent line is another 'foreign' locomotive, a 'WD' 2-8-0.

'County' Class No 1002 *County of Berks* stands in Taunton station with a stopping train for Bristol Temple Meads on 29 June 1947.

On 23 August 1947, 'Castle' Class No 5012 *Berry Pomeroy Castle* heads a Plymouth-North of England express.

Acting as station pilot at Taunton is '14XX' Class 0-4-2T No 5812.

'Bulldog' Class No 3743 *Chaffinch* runs to Taunton loco after arriving with a train from the Barnstaple branch.

Ex-Weston, Clevedon & Portishead Light Railway 0-6-0T No 5 *Portishead* is seen here at Taunton loco on 24 December 1948. Originally purchased from the LBSCR by the WCPR, No 5 came into Great Western ownership in 1940. For several years after the war, together with her sister engine No 6, she was stored out of service at Bristol St Philips Marsh loco until a use was found for her at Taunton.

One of the massive Churchward-built mixed-traffic '47XX' Class 2-8-0s. No 4701, was also photographed at Taunton loco. Mainly used on fast fitted overnight freight trains, they were a fairly rare sighting on daytime duties.

'Counties' at Taunton: No 1008 *County of Cardigan* waits at one of the station's down platforms with a train for Exeter, and on 27 August 1947 No 1026 *County of Salop* is seen at the down main platform.

'51XX' Class 2-6-2T No 4117 backs onto the front of a Paddington-Plymouth express at Taunton to provide assistance over the heavily graded line to Plymouth. The train locomotive is 'King' Class No 6015 *King Richard III*.

'2251' Class 0-6-0 No 2215, coupled to an ROD tender, stands at the west end of Taunton station. This class regularly worked the Minehead and Barnstaple branches.

'Castle' Class No 5066 *Wardour Castle* speeds past Taunton West Junction.

'28XX' Class 2-8-0 No 2808 approaches the west end of Taunton station with an up goods.

Churchward '43XX' 'Mogul' No 6323 approaches Taunton with an up goods train.

'28XX' Class No 2869 is seen at Norton Fitzwarren, west of Taunton, with a lengthy mixed goods train. Norton Fitzwarren was the junction for the Barnstaple and Minehead branches.

South-west of Taunton, at Wellington station, one of the elegant 'Saint' Class 4-6-0s, No 2941 *Easton Court*, pulls away before the ascent of Wellington bank to Whiteball Tunnel and on to Exeter on 19 March 1948.

Climbing towards Whiteball from the other direction is 'Austerity' 2-8-0 No 78717 at Burlescombe with an up goods train on 3 August 1948.

We now follow John to Wales, and at Cardiff General station see '56XX' Class 0-6-2T No 6654 with a Cardiff Valleys train.

Hawksworth-designed 0-6-0PT No 8453 is on another Valleys train at Cardiff General. Although a Great Western design, No 8453 was built by the Yorkshire Engine Company in November 1948.

Collett-designed 0-6-0PT No 5749 is also at Cardiff General station. Built by the North British Loco Company in 1929, No 5749 has the small cab associated with the early engines of this class.

In a complete change of scene we see 'Manor' Class 4-6-0 No 7807 *Compton Manor* at Aberystwyth station with a train for Carmarthen. The smokebox numberplate indicates that this is a post-nationalisation photograph.

Another shot of No 7807 – the location is believed to be Machynlleth loco.

An unidentified 'Dukedog' 4-4-0 stands in Machynlleth station. Originally the 'Earl' Class, the nameplates were removed in pre-war years when members of the House of Lords apparently objected to their titles being associated with such archaic-looking engines. The 'Dukedogs' were rebuilt from 'Duke' and 'Bulldog' Class engines.

Ex-Cambrian Railways 0-6-0 No 849 is at an unidentified location near Machynlleth.

Narrow gauge ex-Vale of Rheidol Railway 2-6-2T No 9 stands at Aberystwyth narrow gauge locomotive sheds.

'57XX' Class 0-6-0PT No 8775 is seen at Yeovil motive power depot.

John's early duties as a Signal & Telegraph apprentice took him to many parts of the South West beyond the Western Region, and these next two photographs were taken on the Southern Region at Yeovil. The first shows lightweight 'West Country' 'Pacific' No 34028 *Eddystone* at Yeovil Junction, and the second mixed-traffic 'S15' Class 4-6-0 No 828 at Yeovil shed, still carrying a Southern Railway number.

4. The Burnham branch of the Somerset & Dorset

Former Midland Railway 0-4-4T No 58046 (No 1298 before renumbering) stands at Highbridge East station (the BR name for the Somerset & Dorset station) with a train for Evercreech Junction on 22 August 1949.

Relative to its size, the S&D has had more books and photographs published about it than many larger railways. However, most of the publications have concentrated on the main line from Bath to Templecombe and Bournemouth, and the branch line to Burnham-on-Sea has been somewhat overlooked.

Highbridge S&D station was actually larger than the adjoining GWR station, having four platforms. The level crossing over the Great Western main line was controlled by the GWR Highbridge West signal box. By the late 1940s passenger traffic to Burnham-on-Sea was light, and freight traffic was made up of movements from Highbridge Wharf to Evercreech and the milk tank traffic to Bason Bridge. I can remember, however, the very early post-war years when passengers changing trains at Highbridge for Burnham on a summer Saturday would find the services packed to overflowing. The luggage/guard's vans would be filled with prams and pushchairs together with babies and their parents – no problems with modern-day health and safety!

Highbridge was home to a fleet of ageing

0-4-4Ts and 0-6-0 tender engines, usually about four of each. On a Sunday there was little or no traffic, so the engine shed was quiet with only a few cleaners and a duty driver present. By and large the drivers were friendly to local enthusiasts and were prepared to move locomotives around the yard for photographic purposes. We were also lucky enough to get footplate trips to Bason Bridge to collect the milk tank traffic. It is surprising how fast a Johnson 0-6-0 would go with the regulator wide open and only a guard's van behind!

Many people did not realise that there were two alternative ways of travelling from Bridgwater to Burnham-on-Sea. The obvious route was via Bridgwater main-line station, changing at Highbridge for Burnham. The other route departed from Bridgwater North (the old S&D station) to Edington Junction, where a change was made to the branch line for Burnham.

The first Ivatt 2-6-2T (No 41241) arrived at Highbridge in February 1950, and this was the beginning of the end for the ageing bogie tanks; similarly the Johnson 0-6-0s were replaced by GWR Collett 0-6-0s, and this in essence was the end of the old S&D. My photographs cover the period 1949-53 and depict the S&D as it looked in its prime.

The beginning of the end for the 0-4-4Ts: on 18 February 1950 Ivatt-designed lightweight 2-6-2T No 41241, after allocation to 22E, waits at Highbridge East station with a train for Evercreech Junction.

Another ex-Midland Railway loco, 0-6-0 No 43593, built in the mid-1880s, has just arrived at Burnham-on-Sea station with a passenger train from Evercreech Junction on 19 August 1950. It is pulling forward from the train and preparing to run round for the return journey to Highbridge. This photograph was taken a few yards from the Bristol Channel; in the early 20th century trucks and wagons would be pushed across the Esplanade and lowered down the jetty for the shipment of goods to Cardiff on the cross-channel ferry.

Ex-Midland Railway 0-4-4T No 58088 (formerly No 1425) stands outside Highbridge loco on 26 November 1950. In the second photograph, now coaled and watered, she is ready for another run across the Somerset Levels to Evercreech.

A powerful engine for the Burnham branch: Fowler 4F 0-6-0 No 44146 stands adjacent to the water tower at Highbridge loco on 4 February 1951. It had just brought in a goods train from Templecombe for Highbridge Wharf.

0-4-4T No 58088 is seen again, at Highbridge East station with a train for Evercreech Junction on 14 April 1951.

On the same day ex-Midland Railway 3F 0-6-0 No 43216 stands at Bridgwater North station with the 3.50pm train for Edington Junction, where the Bridgwater branch joined the Evercreech-Burnham line. It was possible to travel two ways from Bridgwater to Burnham-on-Sea, either from Bridgwater Western Region station, changing at Highbridge, or from Bridgwater North and changing at Edington Junction for the Burnham-on-Sea branch.

One of the original Somerset & Dorset engines, 3F 0-6-0 No 43218, built in 1886, waits at Cossington station on the Edington Junction-Bridgwater branch on 28 April 1951.

Also on 28 April 1951 0-4-4T No 58086 departs from Bason Bridge station, en route to Evercreech. The station was in a very cramped position between the River Brue and the large Express Dairy milk factory. Bason Bridge came to life in the late afternoon when milk tanker wagons were transferred to the main line at Highbridge for onward shipment to London.

Old and new at Highbridge on 17 May 1951: 0-4-4T No 58086 stands 'out of steam' at Highbridge loco, while the second shot shows the first modern locomotive to be allocated to 22E since pre-war days – Ivatt 2P 2-6-2T No 41241 – posing by the water tower. The first Ivatt tank appeared on the branch in early 1950, sounding the death knell for the 0-4-4Ts, which nevertheless soldiered on for several more years.

On 4 August 1951 0-4-4T No 58047 waits for the 'right away' at Highbridge East station with the 10.20am train for Evercreech Junction.

0-4-4T No 58047 in as-built condition with a rounded firebox and a Ross safety valve casing, is photographed in the sun at Highbridge loco on 19 August 1951.

Ex-Midland Railway 3F 0-6-0 No 43419 runs into Highbridge loco after undertaking shunting duties at Bason Bridge on 30 September 1951. The second view captures her at rest in the yard.

Former Midland Railway 3F 0-6-0 No 43792 is attached to an ex-LMS guard's van at Highbridge loco on 25 November 1951. The shed was built as a two-road building, and the second photograph, taken at the rear of the shed on the same day, shows 0-4-4Ts Nos 58086 and 58047 standing 'out of steam'.

These three photographs were taken at Highbridge loco on 3 February 1952. In the first 0-4-4T No 58088 is standing on the coaling line. This low-angle shot emphasises the antiquated appearance of these locomotives.

The second view is of Nos 58072 and 58088 standing together outside the shed. No 58072 has just been allocated to Highbridge and looks immaculate in fully lined-out black livery.

In the final view 0-4-4T No 58072 (formerly No 1379) and ex-SDJR 0-6-0 No 43204 are outside the shed. No 58072 is still fitted with condensing pipes, indicating that at some time she probably worked in the London area.

Ex-Midland Railway 3F 0-6-0 No 43356 is seen outside Highbridge loco on 15 March 1952.

A trip to Evercreech Junction and back on 12 April 1952. 0-4-4T No 58088 is at the head of the 4.13pm train for Evercreech Junction in the bay platform at Highbridge East station.

This photograph was taken from the 4.13pm Highbridge-Evercreech Junction train on 12 April 1952, with 0-4-4T No 58088 at the head, near Ashcott, a small station in the middle of the Somerset Levels. The four-coach train was lightly loaded – half of the passengers, four in number, were members of the 22E Society.

We returned on the 4.34pm West Pennard-Highbridge train, and 0-4-4T No 58072 is on the long straight stretch of track between West Pennard and Glastonbury.

No 58072 runs into Glastonbury station.

At Edington Junction we saw Midland 0-6-0 No 43228 preparing to leave for Bridgwater.

This photograph of 3F 0-6-0 No 43204 at Highbridge loco on 1 June 1952 gives a good view of the primitive coaling stage in the background.

Also seen on 1 June 1952 at Highbridge loco is out-of-service 0-4-4T No 58088, alongside sister loco No 58072, seen in close-up in the second picture.

On 16 August 1952 former Midland Railway 3F 0-6-0 No 43204 stands in Highbridge loco yard.

On the same day another ex-MR 3F, No 43248, departs from Highbridge with a load of empty six-wheeled milk tanks for the Express Dairy factory at Bason Bridge. No 43248 still carries the original 'British Railways' logo on the tender.

By 16 August 1952 Burnham-on-Sea station was closed to regular traffic, but 0-6-0 No 43228 pulls out with a lengthy return Saturday excursion train to Evercreech Junction.

Another ex-Midland Railway 0-6-0, No 43436, is seen standing in Highbridge loco yard on 7 March 1953.

Ex-Midland Railway 3F 0-6-0 No 43216 departs from Highbridge with the 4.13pm train to Evercreech Junction, also on 7 March 1953.

5. The 22E Society

Although this book is intended to portray steam activities in the 1940s and 1950s, it is also a story of schoolboy camaraderie that developed into life-long friendships lasting for more than 60 years. We met as a group of schoolboys on Highbridge station in 1946; John, Roy, Gerald and Tony were the local lads, while Robin and I appeared at school holidays as we spent time at our grandmothers' homes at Highbridge.

Our days were spent on the station platform and as long as we were reasonably well-behaved we had no hassle from the Station Master or Station Foreman. On rainy days we gathered in the down platform waiting room – we were often the only inhabitants, and it had the benefit of a blazing coal fire in the winter. Occasionally we would make trips to Taunton where we could see all the West of England main line express trains.

By 1949/50 changes were taking place within our group of enthusiasts. We were all leaving school and such things as work, higher education, National Service and girlfriends were taking priority. By 1954 our train interests had all but disappeared and apart from occasional meetings between two or three of us and the exchange of Christmas cards we saw very little of each other.

In the early 1960s we were all married and seasonal greetings continued to be the only point of contact, apart from Gerald and I who became brothers-in-law as we married sisters Pauline and Joyce – who said there was no romance in trainspotting? In 1981 one of the group suggested that we all meet up for a reunion, so with our wives we gathered at the Queens Hotel, Burnham-on-Sea, a very appropriate venue as it was adjacent to the now defunct S&D station. At that time we gave the 22E Society its formal title and agreed to meet every year. In 1982 our first get-together was at Stratford-upon-Avon and Warwick Castle – not a train in sight. Thereafter we always met at a preserved railway where we relived our 'spotting days' watched with bemused tolerance by our wives. Sadly, however, in the last few years the 'Great Scrapyard in the Sky' has taken its toll in our ranks, but the 'last of the class' still meet up once a year for lunch and recall the days when 'Steam was King'.

As a matter of interest (hopefully) I conclude with some brief notes on the six members of the 22E Society.

Gerald Buncombe could claim to have 'steam in his blood' as his grandfather, W. W. Buncombe, had a large steam-roller contracting business in Highbridge, alas now all gone, but it is still possible to come across Buncombe's steam-rollers at steam rallies around the country. On leaving school Gerald undertook an engineering apprenticeship, and following National Service joined a large automotive component manufacturing company at Bridgwater where he became a buyer. He married his wife Pauline in 1957.

Roy Medley trained as a pharmaceutical chemist on leaving school, and after qualifying joined Boots the Chemist, eventually becoming a branch manager. In later years he owned his own business in Weston-super-Mare. He married Vicki in 1956. Sadly Roy died in 2003.

Tony Hunt went into the engineering trade on leaving school and was eventually located in the Leeds area. Following in his father's footsteps he formed his own high-tech engineering company making components for the camera industry. Tony is interested in anything mechanical and steam-associated, and is the proud owner of a Burrell showman's engine. He married Enid in 1961, but unfortunately she died in 1998.

John Madeley, a Cornishman by birth, was a Great Western enthusiast to the bitter end – in his opinion no other railway could ever match the GWR. For example, the sight of a Bulleid 'Pacific' or one of the many BR Standard locomotives would leave him completely uninterested. After retiring from BR he spent many years as Signal Engineer with the West Somerset Railway. John married Avril in 1958, and died while still working for the WSR in 2003.

Robin Ward was, like me, a holiday visitor to Highbridge, and after gaining a degree in Mechanical Engineering worked for Metropolitan-Vickers in Manchester. He then joined a major oil company working in the Middle East and the UK. He married Ann in Manchester in 1961.

And I, **John Maybery**, could also claim to have 'steam in my blood', as my great-grandfather, one of his sons and two son-in-laws all worked on the S&D. I trained as an industrial chemist at the National Smelting Company, Avonmouth. After National Service I moved to Frome in Somerset as a chemist and eventually retired as the company's Personnel Director. I married Joyce (Pauline's sister) in 1956.

An early photograph taken on Highbridge station in August 1947. Seated on the down platform are four members of the Society. On the extreme left is a non-member, then Robin Ward, John Maybery, Gerald Buncombe and John Madeley.

Another early photograph, taken on Highbridge up platform in December 1947 – note the GWR logo on the platform seat. Left to right, Roy Medley, John Maybery, John Madeley and Gerald Buncombe. You can see that the standard dress for trainspotters was a blue gabardine raincoat – school caps were optional. Anoraks had yet to arrive on the scene.

The first of our annual reunions was at Leamington Spa in 1983, and this is one of the few photographs we have of everyone and their wives. Back row: Roy, John, John, Avril, Gerald, Robin, Pauline and Tony. Front row: Ann, Enid, Vicki and Joyce.

One Saturday morning in June 1989 'the boys' visited the home of one of John Madeley's WSR colleagues, Vic Boswell, to view his live steam model of a GWR 'County' Class 4-4-0. Left to right: Robin, John, Gerald, Vic, John and Roy.

Llangollen Railway, June 1996: in the cab of GWR 'Hall' Class No 5952 *Cogan Hall* are Gerald and Robin.

Isle of Wight Railway, 1997: gathered around Southern 0-4-4T No 24 are Roy, Pauline, Enid, Gerald, Tony, Ann, Joyce, Vicki and Robin.

North Norfolk Railway, 2001.

Four ageing spotters at the Didcot Railway Centre in May 2002: left to right, Tony, John, Roy and Robin.

The Southern line from Exeter to Okehampton and Plymouth is long closed to passenger traffic, but in 2002 Devon County Council (and other parties) introduced a train/vintage bus service on a circular route to Okehampton-Exeter-Plymouth. Seen here by one of the Devon General vintage buses at Okehampton station are Gerald, Robin and Roy.

Gerald's grandfather, W. W. Buncombe, started a steam-roller contracting business at Highbridge in the early 1900s. Pictured here at Newtown Road, Highbridge, in 1926 are six Babcock steam-rollers being delivered by rail on the S&D – what an impressive 'out of gauge' load! Note the S&D 0-6-0 on the extreme right. W. W. Buncombe is second from the left in the group.

Moving on 84 years, Tony is the proud owner of a Burrell showman's engine, pictured here at a recent event in London. Tony brought his engine down on a low-loader from Leeds and drove it through the streets of London. He is seen in the second view at the controls.

Monday 31 March 86.

Dear Robin and Ann.

Just a brief note to give you a few more details of the w/end April 11/13.

Friday 11th

Suggest you arrive at our house by 7.30 if possible, we have booked accommodation for you at a Guest House, Keyford Elms, about 5 minutes walk from us. I will take you there, suggest you then leave the car there and walk back to us for dinner about 8.30pm.

Saturday 12th

Meet at our house say 10am, we can then go to Bath 'do' the tourist sights, pub lunch and plan to get back to our house late afternoon for tea.

We have booked a table at a local restaurant, and we hope a private room for 8pm. Again within walking distance of our house so no limit on the drink!!

Sunday 13th

Come to the surface! - meet at our house, time to be agreed. Suggestions for Sunday morning: Longleat House/Parkland. Stourhead Gardens or East Somerset Railway.

Lunch at our house.

Looking forward to seeing you on the 11th, don't be late!

Yours.

John & Joyce

Arrangements for our visit to the East Somerset Railway in 1986, and a thematic dinner menu for the 22E Society, prepared for me by a steam enthusiast restaurant owner.

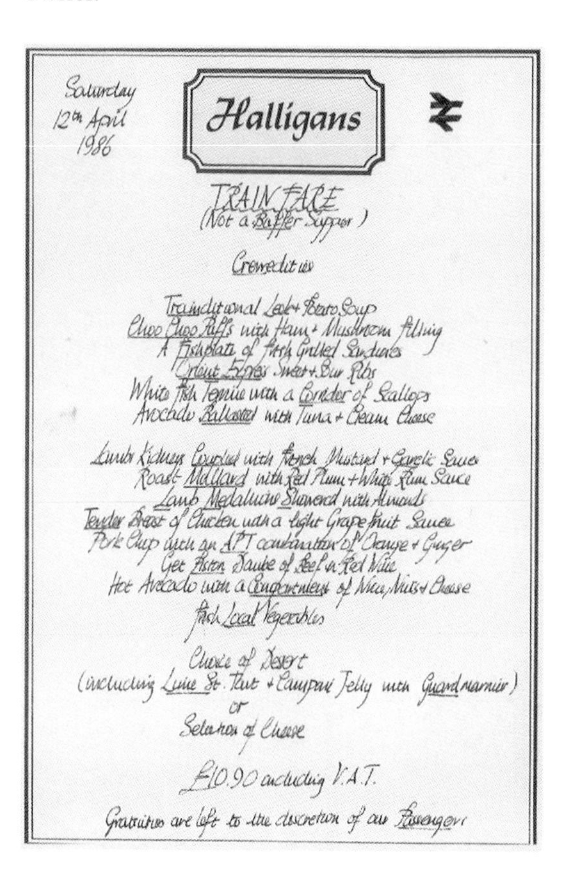

Saturday 12th April 1986

Halligans

TRAIN FARE
(Not a Buffer Supper)

Crewedities

Traindictional Leek + Potato Soup
Choo Choo Puffs with Ham + Mushroom filling
A Fishplate of Fresh Grilled Sardines
Orient Express Sweet + Sour Ribs
White Fish Terrine with a Corridor of Scallops
Avocado Ballasted with Tuna + Cream Cheese

Lamb Kidneys Coupled with French Mustard + Garlic Sauce
Roast Mallard with Red Plum + White Rum Sauce
Lamb Medallions Showered with Almonds
Tender Breast of Chicken with a light Grapefruit Sauce
Pork Chop with an APT combination of Orange + Ginger
Get Aston Daube of Beef in Red Wine
Hot Avocado with a Compartment of Rice, Nuts + Cheese
Fresh Local Vegetables

Choice of Desert
(including Lime St. Tart + Campari Jelly with Grandmarnier)
or
Selection of Cheese

£10.90 including V.A.T.

Gratuities are left to the discretion of our Passengers

22 SOCIETY

27 April 1992

Dear Robin & Ann.

Biggin Hall Week-end

Enclosed map on how to find Biggin Hall plus various leaflets which you might find interesting, even though they are dated 1991! We had a local reunion here last month, so now everyone has all details. You will have to move to the South West and join us!

Just a reminder that we are eating in the hotel both evenings and dinner is at 7.00pm, with party games afterwards, only pulling your leg Ann.

Looking forward to seeing you on Friday 12 June, we aim to arrive mid-afternoon.

Kind regards from us both.

Joyce

A 22E Society letterhead arranging a visit to the Midland Railway Centre and Crich Tram Museum, 1992.

Index of locations

Further reading...

Before his sudden death in 2000 Gerald Adams had planned this book, and Silver Link is pleased to honour this lifelong railway enthusiast and photographer by bringing his project to fruition. During the 1950s and '60s Gerald lived in Birmingham, then Gloucester, so his book was intended to bring together photographs he had taken within or just outside his three favourite counties, Worcestershire, Herefordshire and Gloucestershire – the 'Cathedral Counties', as he called them.

Here, then, are more than 280 pictures, of remote, rural branch lines and busy railway centres like Birmingham and the county cities of the three shires. They also cover many rail tours, sadly marking the closure of lines and withdrawal of locomotives classes in that momentous last decade of steam on Britain's railways.

Size:	**238 x 172mm**	**ISBN:**	**978 1 85794 350 4**
Extent:	**160pp**	**Format:**	**Hardback**
Illustrations:	**c280 b/w**	**RRP:**	**£25.00**

SLP

Silver Link Publishing Ltd

The Trundle, Ringstead Road, Great Addington, Kettering, Northamptonshire NN14 4BW

Tel/Fax: 01536 330588 email: sales@nostalgiacollection.com Website: www.nostalgiacollection.com